SILENCE *of the* COUNTRY

SILENCE *of the* COUNTRY

KRISTJANA GUNNARS

COTEAU BOOKS
WWW.COTEAUBOOKS.COM

Edited by Geoffrey Ursell.

Cover image: Emily Carr, *Wood Interior,* 1932-1935, oil on canvas, 130.0 X 86.3 CM,
Vancouver Art Gallery, Emily Carr Trust, VAG 42.3.5 (Photo: Trevor Mills)

Cover design by Tania Wolk, Magpie Design.
Book design by Duncan Campbell.

Printed and bound in Canada at Transcontinental Printing.

National Library of Canada Cataloguing in Publication Data

Gunnars, Kristjana, 1948-
Silence of the country

Poems.
ISBN 1-55050-202-6

I. Title.
PS8563.U574S54 2002   C811'.54   C2002-910314-2
PR9199.3.G793S54 2002

1   2   3   4   5   6   7   8   9   1 0

COTEAU BOOKS   AVAILABLE IN THE US FROM
401-2206 Dewdney Ave.   General Distribution Services
Regina, Saskatchewan   4500 Witmer Industrial Estates
Canada   S4R 1H3   Niagara Falls, NY 14305-1386

The publisher gratefully acknowledges the financial assistance of the
Saskatchewan Arts Board, the Canada Council for the Arts, the Government of
Canada through the Book Publishing Industry Development Program (BPIDP),
and the City of Regina Arts Commission, for its publishing program.

contents

Introduction – i

city fog – 3
old gifts – 4
chestnut blossoms – 5
cloud cover – 6
the wet shade of old firs – 7
in the afternoon – 8
street corner – 9
silence of the country – 10
Port Stalashen – 11
mid-winter dusk – 12
after Amsterdam – 13
trickster – 14
city traffic –15
Sunday afternoon – 16
Arctic cathedral – 17
millennium – 18
later that night – 19
at the beach – 20
Georgia O'Keeffe – 21
quiet of the morning – 22
La Réunion – 23
forecast – 24
country living – 25
Rundetårn – 26
ink stains – 27

ashes and wax – 28

tire tracks – 29

day in court – 30

confession – 31

new year's eve – 32

picture window – 33

at the Grand Café – 34

morning after – 36

tonight's weather – 37

Mary's apartment – 38

a word from London – 39

Valentine's Day – 40

shooting range – 41

the years – 42

the compass – 43

winter gales – 44

the long afternoon – 45

the other way – 46

Krokskogen – 47

the real postmodern – 48

the two rivers – 49

the book of life – 51

exterminator – 52

calling card – 53

holiday – 54

the message – 55

Acknowledgements – 57

Introduction

This collection of poems was written after I lived in Norway for half the year of 1997. Oslo was expensive. Housing cost twice as much as in Canada, and luxuries we take for granted like restaurant meals in North America are sky high in Scandinavia. It was a wake-up call to have no money, and not to be able to carry on with simple things in life. But for me there was more to adjust to. The Norwegian language has so many dialects that you can never be sure which one you will hear when you meet someone. For me it was like being partially deaf. Large patches of conversation would simply fall out of my hearing because I did not understand the dialect. It was a debilitating experience to be without a language half the time again. For a writer, that is a serious problem. Added to the standard of living and the language, all the issues of migration attended my stay. The absence of community, friends, a grounding in society, made my life in Norway a challenge I was not ready for, coming as it did in the middle of life.

But Norway fascinated me. I travelled when I was there, and every new place opened up areas of the imagination I had not encountered before. The western seaside town of Bergen, perched on the mountainsides, with a language sounding so much like my native Icelandic. The barren plateaus around Trondheim, with wild elk racing across the vista and the landscape dotted with wooden farmhouses all painted white or red. The amazing placement of the northern town of Tromsø, which was an embarking point for northern exploration. The great polar explorers set off from Tromsø, and their memorabilia can be found in the town. Then the placid pasture-like settings of southern Norway, the green undulating landscape, with its valleys and seaside towns. The old factory tenements dotting the eastern seascape, places of common people with proletarian histories. And the magnificent estates that can be found now and then, such as Eidsvold.

A friend of mine once said when you leave home and spend a long time in a foreign place, you lose your centre. I did not think I would lose my centre in Norway. After all, I was born and raised in that part of the world, and after living in Norway I can much better understand the culture I came from myself, since Iceland was built on Norwegian foundations. But nonetheless, I did lose my grounding. Soon I felt utterly lost. Every day I awoke and wondered where I was and why I was there. Nothing seemed recognizable. I forgot how to write altogether. I had a computer and a desk and time, but I no longer knew how to write. It was like losing my ability to pursue my craft. Like being a carpeneter and no longer knowing how to build a cabinet or a table. Like being a weaver and no longer remembering how a loom works. It was as if I had lost all my tools in the transition.

After finding myself completely unskilled again, with the memory of all the learning that had gone into the creation of a text becoming a faint star in the morning sky, I latched onto the only thing I had left: reading. Instead of doing the regular activities I had become used to, I spent nearly all my time reading books, when we were not travelling somewhere. I found all the bookstores within the range of trains and buses around my house. It was at that time that I read all of Maurice Blanchot. I read Walter Benjamin. I read philosophy texts I found in the University bookstore. I read books on psychology and sociology. It was an experience that reminded me of when I was very young, suddenly new in Canada, and living in a place in BC where I knew no one. I discovered Duthie Books and read and read and read until the world seemed right again.

But we returned to Canada, to my home in BC, and I started piecing my life together again. In a very strange way, I felt as though I had gone into outer space and could not be sure my own world, the earth and its trees and birds, would still be there when I returned. I did not understand the simplest things about this process, such as the strange conceptualization of time that goes on. Because you return home to a place you imagine has stood still in time, and you have been away in a pocket of your own, and a time zone not shared by anyone you know. Your friends and relatives are people who suddenly seem strangers to you. They have to be discovered all over again.

I went about the house and the yard and the environment refamiliarizing myself with everything. I had to more or less move into my own home anew. I set up my computer and my writing pad and told myself I could write whatever I wanted. There would be no censoring of anything. I could go over those months in Norway at whatever pace I liked, and write myself back into my own existence. For the next three years, I carved out poem after poem, at a rather slow pace. I noticed the poems were hard at the edges. They refused to become soft and pliable. I wrote them as if I had just learned English again. All this was strange, since I had already published six books of poems, not to mention the prose books I had authored. Every poem was as if chiselled out of stone. I felt like the carver of runes on those old stone slabs, declaring in a cumbersome alphabet with unskilled hands and a dearth of carving tools, that I am here and I am a writer. Because if you are a writer, there is no way of not being one. It has nothing to do with whether you are a good or a bad writer. You just are. Your medium is language, the way the musician lives in the medium of sound.

These are the poems that tell the tale of returning, written in the quietude of rural BC as they remember other places and other times and try to understand the changes that have occurred. They are hard won, and paid for with what feels like a heavy personal price. So much can be lost in the kinds of transitions mine represented. Identity, culture, language, all are on the chopping block. I had to write myself back to myself, and every poem is a step forward. I tried to recall the moments in Norway that had made an impression on me, and to think about the tricks memory can play, even when remembered moments are clear as glass. In the end, what emerged is a bit like an Indian cotton cloth with tiny mirrors sewed in all over. The little mirrors here and there, individual poems stuck into the fabric of the West Coast backdrop, are odd moments remembered, reflected from my time in Norway.

SILENCE *of the* COUNTRY

city fog

since life has become so prosaic
fog everywhere, a few leaves
left on the alders, a slim outline
of tall treetrunks in the mist
branch out into the pale morning
faded and delicate, the lace of earth

how the clock keeps its own time
without regard for the rest of us, our nerves
shake out the day like so much linen
so without the least poetic wing
nothing in flight now, all things dim
only the smitten raccoons like rats

scurry for bits of bread in the park
where the ruthless feed them, the blind
bicyclists who cannot read signs
play with those rabid mouths at night
below the precipice of the Sound
before the lights of the city go out

old gifts

those four silver goblets, how
they always go dark, tarnished
in the vacuum of time, whenever I look
they stand unmoved

how I wanted to polish and drink
wine from those mouths
and year after year never did
even decades later their rims unused

they just stand on the table
potential and taunting, as if the hint
itself were better than nothing
a gleam of silver draped in neglect

chestnut blossoms

Because it was a song they sang in the fifties:
chestnut trees blossoming in Bygdøy Allé,
Oslo, that long boulevard of open dreams
lined with crowned anticipations, small
flowers chasing the breeze off the sea;

and because I took to that dark street, with
its antique stores, interior design, old movie
theatres, cafés for the lost and lonely; and
because it became a boulevard of dashed hopes
or a place I rarely visited except when sad,

I never saw the spring blossoms, the ones
they sang about, so late in spring already
when I arrived. For me only the green crowns
of things accomplished before me, inheritances
I alone could say I did not want.

cloud cover

it is not the low-lying clouds over the water
the transparently white air, like seeing through glass
the kind your breath is on when your lips touch the pane
those clouds, goose-down white and thick with perfume
of wet cedar, soggy maple leaves, the debris of fall

or even when the clouds are so low I see above them
from my desk looking out, the cloud cover under the window
like you do in airplanes when landing, the long glide down
onto some runway glistening in the newly fallen rain
you coming out of your reverie, your delusion of sky

I know it is not the comforting cloud blanket, plumes
of smoke from the neighbour's chimney sliding up
between the tall fir trees and spindly alders, haze
of burning logs drifting up as if it were a ghost:
but something quite other, something harder to see

the wet shade of old firs

in spite of that, dinner bread already
before eleven rises on the stove with walnuts,
raisins, apples inside, the fire burns
through a damp West Coast morning
old logs dry in the wicker basket, in spite of

chamomile tea in mugs, berber
cushions by the woodstove flames
nice details of domestic life in the country
the pleasant smell of woodsmoke, long
silence of rainy days and foggy afternoons –

yet the underbrush quails, hemlock
branches co-mingle outside the study
window, dank brown leaves of maple
cover up for field mice and long-legged spiders
and forty or fifty ladybugs nest in the door

in the afternoon

the morning run, taken between four
and five in the afternoon, when sun is low
in November, evening lilacs emerge
over hills of the fjord, my sneakers
just warm enough for the cold street, back
and forth, down Deertrail Road, Sandy
Shores Road, Deertrail Road again, up
Mt. Tetrahedron Road and back again

the same way another time and
another, always another round
my Kahlua sweatsuit just thick enough
to absorb the film of sweat, especially
uphill, the calves of my legs burn
I imagine at every corner I could run
away, to some place I have never seen
where hyacinths stay blue all year

street corner

three drunks shout in animated conversation about art
young women sell white lace dresses for a romantic
occasion that never comes, in Tromsø

they dream, the wine stores overflow, the cafés
are run by former Yugoslavians, the consumers
are tourists from the other continents, in Tromsø

to see polar bears on the streets, to check out
shipwrecks from Arctic explorations, to discover
what happpens to the soul after hermiting the North

silence of the country

I tell myself this is home
remind myself, as if otherwise
forgotten, a memory blackout, so I say

my oakwood table, my white office lamp
from the village store, my pictures
the ones I ask no one else to like

my stained glass windows on chains
even the green beeswax candles, mine
in brass candelabras with long legs

as if it could be taken away, perhaps by love
or some twist of fate
it has often been said nothing is secure

not even the view, the still
vision of Mount Khartoum, snow-
dusted green hills going down

into mauve water, not even this
vision from my window is sure
and I knock on the glass to hear a sound

Port Stalashen

Even though it was Indian land
no one else could own, they built a hundred
and thirty condos, made a false beach
fenced with bricks, dumped grey sand
below the end window, the cupola-
shaped glass some Californians, she said

bought for six hundred thou but only live in
a couple of months a year, pink and yellow
vinyl siding, small balconies
in the shade. Even though
the gravel walk was slip-
shod, the cement tiles wobbly

and the false marina too new, two
small boats already moored there
with the shaved off hills behind, carved
for the gravel mines. Oversized conveyor
belts moved the soil into Georgia
Strait. Construction and empty homes

with no one living anywhere, all for show.
Old beach houses lay crowded
in by lumber trucks and concrete
mixers and the noise of hammers all day.
And when we looked south, hundreds of
white gulls rose in unison to the sky.

mid-winter dusk

The deck chairs are folded and lie
face down on the cedar planks, the rocking
chair upside down, its rocker legs poking
into the mid-winter air. On the railing

a film of rime from the night, water-
coloured and glassy on the blue paint.
The two pegs that went missing in summer
now nailed down against winter gales,

that come in off the Pacific, from
November to March, great gusts that turn
their way down the fjord. The umbrella
pole still sticks up from the garden

table, its base in a load of rocks
picked from the yard, before the lawn
came in. Droplets have formed on top
to mark the melting of morning frost

and the beginning of late afternoon. All
colours so pastel, so flush with lilac
and silk, and when the gusts die, with satin,
as if to say good night in a cold bed.

after Amsterdam

On the plane from Amsterdam, a movie
showed the Oscar de la Renta of cooking,
a fat man in his fifties, white hair, thick
fingers, walking through the regions of Italy
in the north. Talking about basil.

Basil, he said, is the heart of Italy, is
the blood of the earth, pungent and green
and profuse. The mortar and pestle, he
said, the tools of life itself. And he churned
the dark basil leaves in olive

oil, in pine nuts off the hills, in garlic
cloves and thick parmesan. We remembered
that film as in a dream we had
when flying away from our castaway troubles
going home. At home, I said to him,

we have our own. Every Saturday still
we open a Chianti for the pasta pesto,
we remake the day we flew over Amsterdam
and into Vancouver. We remember
the future we came all this way to create.

trickster

stellar jays jump from branch to branch
as if the rain did not matter, as if
the drops that fall were not too big
for those steel blue feathers, those black
top hats they wear all the time

as if the tin-coloured sky were not too
thick for their small eyes, and the trees
too nude now, too scraggled with the few
crumpled brown leaves that hang on
well into next spring, as if the highest

spinny aldertop were not too high
when the wind begins to blow, when
the big ravens descend from the beach
with the over-confident air they have
that they are the deified ones here

city traffic

when the chestnut trees blossom in Bygdøy
I want to be far away, I want the thin
white flowers to come and go without me

I tell myself it would be all too heavy
the concrete and steel of Oslo town too
hard on the eyes, sharp in the corners

and days I slip into buildings
for the comfort of wood, the gentle play
of light in small windows, the warm aroma

of coffee somewhere, or low conversation
always end too soon and the streets
are always too hard for my thin shoes

and the small blossoms stay too short
like a breath in the night, they wash past
as if they too have to rush somewhere else

Sunday afternoon

that fierce undertow that says I want
to be free, how tough it is, how sudden
the springs go loose, and the sea itself
unable to hold back the rising tides

for when we walked on the pebbled
beach of Davis Bay, we saw those logs out
on the water in thousands, I said a chain
around a boom must have broken

the towboat helpless as tree-
trunks floated everywhere in the Strait
washing up on marinas and sandpiles
in the chaos of voluminous rains

and I saw the chains of the heart itself
go loose and snap, the many moments
of doubt go free, and the tears too
and the harsh current from below

Arctic cathedral

In the ice cathedral of Tromsø they had
to replace the hills of western Norway
with Jesus Christ, for the simple reason
the mountains were too stark, the light

coming in from the east too bright. Through
the clear glass it shone directly into eyes
of parishioners on their benches. When
they looked up at the priest they saw nothing

but a bath of light from the midnight sun.
The architect's design, to bring nature herself
into the service, went by the wayside, glass
artists were called to make a stained picture

window showing Christ on the cross, and now
we cannot see the barren fells of the north
even from the front row. But we do see
the face of the priest, the coloured glass in blue

and yellow, the otherwise bare white walls
of something they say should be an iceberg.
And we, small creatures, mob inside
in an ocean of blue, a sea of purple light.

millennium

the slow frost of morning and pink
December clouds, the sun low before solstice

we are looking at the end of the millennium
tired of that line, that thought, long before

the century changes, a cliché already
because the thin rime of the West will be

the same then as now, the maroon sun-
set show no change, the way we count

days and years our only alibi, our slim
knowledge of mathematics all our faith

I tell myself this, leafing through the papers
left in boxes when my father died, child

of this century, I say sometimes, born
at the start, he had the grace to die

before we came to this, the last lining
of the last tin-coloured cloud of dawn

later that night

Darkness comes seldom these days. High
winds find their way between branches, deep
rain covers the red cedars, and in all the view

to the end of no horizon, only fog or mist
fades into greys and purples. Night never
falls any more, too often beset by moon-

light stronger than sun, the air outside
the window lit in a neon of space. I think of
moon-bathers in their pink saris, the surprise

every time I pull the white curtain slightly
aside, the one that trails along the bedroom
floor, and find no darkness, once again.

at the beach

since no special days are better than others
the blue shale of Høvik beach, sometimes hot
light of a midday sun, black and white striped
strand chairs we use to lean back in

a slight breeze off the Oslofjord, cool enough
to keep us in place, gentle enough not to blow
pages of *Aftenposten* or *The New York Review
of Books* we throw on the rocks beside us

into the air, where an endless din of jet planes
comes and goes on the tarmac of Fornebu
Airport and drills into the silence of our afternoons
that too is ordinary, never a change in the two-

minute interval between aircraft, or the number
of sailboats on the tin-blue water, or the nature
of ripples tickling the legs of our beach chairs
just like that, nothing special, nothing better

Georgia O'Keeffe

so I look for signs where I can take refuge
everything turns outward, like petals
of a giant orchid that unfolds, perhaps a Georgia
O'Keeffe painting in bright orange

my days turned out to someone else
he sits across from me at the butcher block
bowl of coffee in his hands, he walks with me
in the village, picks out apples and tomatoes

at the Galiano Produce Market, collects old
bottles for recycling in the bin that has stood
under the counter for years now, suddenly
he is the one who chops wood for the stove

and he is the one who speaks on the phone
and takes in mail from the post office
and negotiates with my friends, the one
to whom all things are turned, like the sun

quiet of the morning

as I stand here kneading dough, whole
wheat flour, caraway seeds, dill seeds, Irish
Breakfast Tea steeps in the old pot
the first porcelain after marriage, thirty

years ago now and gone, the dinner ticket
for New Year's Eve is in the napkin holder
flimsy wicker from the Chinese variety store
on Cowrie Street, and a calling card from someone

named Sally at Trinkets & Treasures, who says
she will buy all my little objects
when I leave this house and move overseas
where my beach chairs lie folded in shed four

nineteen in Drammen, and the milk swirls
around in the flour, the wooden spoon
laps edges of the big pasta bowl, as I stand here
and the ocean outside goes slack

La Réunion

It cannot escape me that I am not the first
to go this way, as if going were enough,
as if direction were all. A black raven glides past
my big window, I see the feathers below,

dim and steel-coloured in the early dawn. On
the water huge treetrunks float, ones that have come
loose in the latest storm and been swept to sea
by waves persistent as time. Continuous

in their unfolding, they say only in La Réunion
do ocean waves break to the left. There the waters
of high peaks fall down in thin stripes, into canyons
laced with brightly coloured foliage I do not

recognize. But today we are all quiet. On the glass
top of the table, a book of poems by Edith
Sødergran prompts me. On the bamboo shelf,
a biography of Georgia O'Keeffe. Increased isolation

was not just mine. Yellow flats of sunlight do not
lie on the mountains I see alone, above the clouds
in their heaviness. There are others, I tell myself,
there must be others as the sea lights up.

forecast

I think there are days without weather
even though there is always air and always moisture
and usually there are clouds somewhere
folding themselves around a hilltop, say

but the days when air and water do not move
when the sea is neither glassy nor in ripples
when the clouds are neither high nor low
and the sun not there, not not there

those are days without weather, ennui days
when I wander through the hallway of my house
like a ghost in my own life, when I find myself
staring into the calm afternoon

cold but not cold, too warm for a fire
too chilly for a hike in the heritage trails
they cut through the wood last November
and I wish there were rain to erase it all

country living

every time we walk past Irene's log cottage
the dogs bark madly, all four of them
big as lions, white, red, brown, and down below
Ken who puts on the Santa suit at Christmas
lives behind a pile of rocks, and underneath

the great Sequoia tree Lee and Bonnie run the tap
for afternoon tea today too, and on the corner
the nameless fellow with a sign that says TIMBER
supports this family, covers his property with lights
of all colours, because December is here again

and the nearly bald Dorothy from the hillside
house on stilts is seen once again on the run
all nine klicks to the village along a winding road
in her shiny leotards and runners, her nice husband
waiting in the car at the gates to the Reservation

where none of the white folks are allowed to go
anyway, but the neighbourhood carries on
the same day after day, cats out on the prowl
until they are eaten by bobcats, and they in turn
by cougars, and the bears have gone to sleep

and snowflakes slowly tumble, large and soggy
from the clouds, and an occasional black helicopter
breaks the windless noonday, and rumours
of whales have come around again, a pod is passing
in the waters of the milk-white Strait

Rundetårn

today we look over the city from on top
of the old Tower they say dated back
to the Renaissance, to days when astronomy
sounded like postmodernism does now

from this angle all the tile-stoned rooftops
of Copenhagen are rust-brown, clotheslines
hold up the day's wash between buildings, flower
pots line the railings of tiny balconies

and on the narrow streets below they say
seventy thousand people mill about, security
guards stand on other rooftops, fences
have been constructed to block whole avenues

since the American President is also here today
he is going to speak to multitudes on Strøget
perform for the Danish people and all others
in town today, each for their own reasons

and it is only the second time I visit the Round
Tower, this time I am grown, my flowered
skirt, white sneakers and bright orange sweater
say nothing of who I have become in this crowd

ink stains

because I have been thinking of slaves
the many ways we can become one

how the day enslaves us, dawn
seeps into the night like red ink

dogs begin to bark in the neighbourhood
the light at the gravel pit blinks

those who work for others sail out
to the mine in a deep drone

of engines that cut in unnatural ways
the silence of the purple morning

our long complaints absorb themselves
into our brains like moisture

how I wish the sun would turn pink
and take away the dark thought

that says I too am in the family of slaves
and the stillness of the palace

ashes and wax

so the holidays are done
so guests have taken their overcoats
the big black shoes by the front door
and they have headed off on the boat that plies the sound

the umbrellas hang politely again
on the front door shelving, all the rain
water dripped away overnight
and the beds with crumpled sheets stand emptied in rooms

quiet returns like a thief in the night
we awake to the disappearance of things
tabletops suddenly empty, hangers naked
and a vacuum we now fill with the breath of ourselves

tire tracks

and we are here like two old people, old
before our years, off in the fog
that accompanies being on the earth
too long perhaps, too intent on one narrative
one story that makes a life, and now

we have sent them all into their own
pockets of life, in their own worn sneakers
and second hand rain jackets, unkempt
and in wrinkled shirts they went off
to make sounds of their own, young sounds

and we look at each other across the old
Mexican table, once again only two
clay plates, the last two wine glasses left
after all the others have broken
and some Okanagan Merlot on a cork plate

we pass the evening in quiet like that
cold fog rises from the water
filling in the last patch of starlight
the last chorus of winter birds swings
to the west and nothing more moves

day in court

sometimes memory deceives, they say
it often does, like an incompetent witness
who could not hear and could not see
and got the dates wrong and the facts wrong

cards, say, that trickled in with the post
cheerful greetings from old friends, one
by one they lined up on the top shelf
behind the dining table, soon so many

and the laptop from Mac & Carry, all
those emails pouring in, day after
day through a small device some young
curly-haired virtuoso arranged

and dinner parties now stashed
away in the brain, dressed-up folks
with earrings and polished shoes in loud
conversation around the rosewood-veneered

table we rented in those days, silly
IKEA sofas in the corners, old wine-glass
cabinets with glass doors and keys
our old rented life, half-remembered

as harsh and lonely, strangers
everywhere and hard feelings, perhaps
it was just my own judge of a mind
that would not allow the evidence in

confession

Angus Creek is full of carcasses now
dead salmon washed downstream after spawning
we stand on the footbridge in the smell of rot
speckled bodies splayed along the banks

and I think of the folktale of someone
who confessed her secret to the river
just to tell it somewhere, that nagging knowledge
you know will someday rear itself up

out of the waters, a prehistoric monster
mythified over time, like Lochness perhaps
or the Lagarfljót Worm or Bigfoot in the Cascades
maelströms we want to tell our secrets to

new year's eve

then I look at him in his Indian
cotton vest with the Nehru collar
a yellow logger shirt from the Northwest
his combed hair, blond after all

and I think it could not be me he loved
but rather a new life, something
he desired for himself, something
that seemed to fit in the course of his years

sad reflections perhaps, like the reluctant
drops of rain on the railing
outside the kitchen window, how they fall
heavily on the blue paint

and form small puddles on the cedar
while the white air gathers more
the world in a sheen of water
a film that covers everything

picture window

I found a postcard in an old pile of papers.
I remember when I brought it home,
many years ago, from a shop on Whyte Avenue.
A card that shows a window alcove
with yellow pillows and paprika coloured rugs
with curtains. Outside is a blue sky
with trees around the edges, green lawns
and an inlet of deep blue water in the sun.
It was where I wanted to be then.
Somewhere, anywhere, other than this snow,
I said. And now I am there. Outside,
the blue water is often white from clouds.
The sun often disappears in a band of rain.
The green hillsides turn purple so easily
and there really are no lawns. It is raining
most of the time. My neighbour across the street
takes pills for depression. My other neighbour
knits the blues away and has many sweaters.
Be careful what you covet, they say,
for you might get it. If your desires materialize,
be careful how you use them. I now have new
binoculars on my desk. When something irks,
I take them up and look out to the horizon.
There specks of dust turn into large boats.
Black minutiae in the sky become bald eagles.
Small huts along the water's edge become mansions,
and I know it was not an illusion.

at the Grand Café

In the corner Henrik Ibsen's old table
stands, his top hat and his gloves lie
folded on the round marble, his walking
stick leans on the chair, a menu
open on the dinner plate, still set
for the man who can no longer come here

because he is dead. All his associates
are also dead. Bjørnsterne Bjørnson,
Edvard Munch, Knut Hamsun. All the old
artists of Oslo, dead and gone. A time
long passed. At the Grand Café where once
they congregated, only a mural

painted on the wall commemorates.
Here Ibsen, they say, drank his routine
four glasses of wine every evening, enjoyed
dinner, society. The men and women
had affairs with one another across
marriages, and sailed out on rowboats

together to declare their love, in summer
when weather was good. Politicians
stood up from tables and chewed each other
out along with duck meat and pigeon
meat and the occasional lutefisk. Now
the old place is full of the bourgeoisie

trying to be part of a lost Atlantis.
Real artists have gone elsewhere, they
say, and the old Café is for tourists. I too
have been lured here many times. White
lunch wine, flamboyant sandwiches,
extravagant deserts. And then again

a walk home in the rain in wet shoes
and a useless umbrella, goodbye hugs
on the steps of the University Library
where pink-faced law students prowl.
What is left of Norway's golden days,
a series on TV, and cement-coloured rain.

morning after

how yesterday's flowers rearrange themselves
they all lean towards the window

how every morning the snow-dusted peaks
bathe in peach-coloured sunlight

and the rugged water, how that too
stops mirroring raven wings in the wind

winter mornings in the West, how seldom
such crispness, such sun, such light

how transfixed I am, the coffee grows cold
in my cup, I find myself dreaming

at the kitchen window, the bouquet
orange, purple, blue on the table

where yesterday we said goodbye, some-
how parting at the break of day

tonight's weather

no one promised you a whisper
a hope, a tree to lean on, nothing

not even the brush of a seagull's wing
against your wet cheek

I tell myself such cold stories, ice
rain everywhere, electricity gone

a hearsay of the land I live in
a breath I did not even feel

in what I see is a pocket of world
stopped in its tracks by the unsaid

an undiscovered coastline, without
roads or paths or even maps

where I can call to no hearing
and ask so strange questions

of the earth, such as do I live
and not a whisper echoes

Mary's apartment

a Mother Mary night light in the hall
dimly glows its dime-store plastic
on a faded red carpet, the cat inside
drinks water from the toilet bowl
specks of kitty litter on the bathroom floor
Donald Duck grins on the bathtub rim

on the kitchen sink a naked baby
soap dish holds its bar of Ivory
plastic-wrapped collages on the walls
where bad art in rich gold frames hangs
old newspapers in piles on the floor

I walk about my friend's pad stoically
pretending I belong in her eclectic
world with its baby crib and teethers
pretend the windows are airtight
and do not let in the damp Vancouver

cold, thick falling snow outside
reflects in the streetlights of English
Bay and piles up on car hoods
while I turn the heat up to full
clockwise on the floor radiators

a word from London

in the bleak midwinter
frosty wind made moan
earth stood hard as iron
water like a stone

for where to begin and where to end is unknown
where to turn when one hundred thousand per day

find the homeless shelter in London
whether it is the same hundred thousand or not

each time the river flows anew
the same water every day made fresh again

this Sunday morning when the clouds are bleak
and nothing stirs in the alder branches

I wish I could sleep under the cloudless sun
and it looks like early tulips already bow down

Valentine's Day

because the clouds have not passed all day
because the rain falls and does not fall
and the light goes soft in the afternoon
becomes the tincture of blueberry by four

the water sweet with white-granuled sky
marbles itself in swirls and blotches
and the evening is grey as woodfire smog
people rest their purple hearts now

I do not think I was made for this rose
not pink, not orange, but black in its vase
a romantic gift once meant for Valentine
but romance, he says, is ideology in white

and I admit the ocean in the fjord looks cold
has the aura of an unwanted skin disease
and the clouds above, bruised purple
how they hang their rags out to dry

shooting range

to say I wanted that other life
the past always goes off somewhere else
the balloon meant to take them around the world

ends up in strips on the canyon floor
I wanted first the quiet of Sunday afternoon
the African violet that opens to itself in one place

vermilion I can count on as vermilion
a pebbled walkway to my own brass-fitted door
and nothing extra to take the hours from my oak clock

I know I dream the dreams of grief
when you have lost what you never had
such easy misses in the target practice of dawn

the years

suddenly I park near the grocery door
I buy cheap now, two for the price of one
even lottery tickets and beer in cans
all my former principles up in smoke

along with today's newspaper and old bills
still unpaid on the desk top
life changes I tell them all
one day you find yourself a stranger

blowing kisses to the wind
devil-may-care if all this is new
old Christmas cards line the inside ledge
long into February now

suddenly I look in the mirror
some face there I did not know before
the color of those eyes unrecognizable
maybe green or grey

and there is a draw about the neck
muscles I did not know were there
of course grey hairs in the eyebrows
and golden half-moons on the floor

the compass

like that I would take a star from the night sky

slip it on my finger long before morning

take a stroll through pictures in a children's book

one with pale horses and mountains and lakes

like that I would dream myself awake

I cover my eyes with my palms to see if I can

do not turn the lights on when dusk falls

listen to the sound all this silence makes

put my ear to the ground to hear horses' hooves

I am not alone in this the cedar branches tell

especially when the wind blows they come clean

purity is something only mountain peaks achieve

the angelic is only found in the white wake of boats

and I navigate solely on instinct by now

winter gales

winter does not yield its hand
though jaybirds flourish wings throughout
January days and February days in defiance
storms are in and continue to rage

on such days I think winter dances
movement, action, never-silencing
the face of the clock speeds up in distress
wind, it says, and goes around fast

speed of lightning in my throat
many motions I made myself to speak
every day I awaken to unsaid lines
there is never enough time again

water stagnates in its clay jug
on the table where I left it, aeons ago
water everywhere now, pours
as if nothing else is

the long afternoon

lilies, lavender and white
as in wedding bouquets, some misunderstanding
will not die in the vase
weeks go by, hard
winter days, the wood stove crackles
metal pops, flames
rush in an angry draft, still
flowers stand up in the air

heat from cast iron lingers
after the fire is out, coals in ashes
simmer on heatproof bricks
the day barely begun when it ends
ourselves so long married
even wild boars are bored with us
raccoons and skunks waddle to lairs
and leaves of old books turn

the other way

I tell you small things

a pebble in my shoe

a piece of cracker on the kitchen floor

a grain of dust in my eye

larger discomforts I dare not voice

a rainbow over the valley

that ends and ends and ends

I tell you there is no gold

Krokskogen

in an old forest cottages stand
among twisted birches and firs, cows
with bells on rummage among roots
and trunks, goats jump

rocks jutt up from gravel
a succession of paths mountaineers take
looking for old answers
in footsteps of folklore gatherers

the seter culture of Norway
lies in echo around the bend
girls sent to spend summers with livestock
in the hills beyond thought

the real postmodern

The top brass button on my blue velvet coat
fell off. The button is in the pocket
and the coat hangs unused on an old hanger.
When I wear that old thing I am aware
the button is missing. The picture is flawed.

A coat once interesting, now old. Bought
on my arrival in the town of Edmonton.
Prairie bird that I was, landing there
blue and brass, protected against the cold.
Now time has caught up with us both,

and I can tell you in all confidence
the coat is going to St. Mary's Auxiliary,
a gift for a depleted hospital, a thrift shop special
someone else can wear in the months
ahead. I am going to West Edmonton Mall

to buy a new coat. A bright, shiny covering
to wear in the town of Oslo, so far away.
I know I can change identities the way
you can change coats, and I am Norwegian now.
It was not as hard to do as you might think.

You and I both know identity
is a nebulous thing. The world does not turn
along the ways we have defined its path.
The world just turns. The world just is.
And we in it are always able to live.

the two rivers

Over the prairies the air is thick with
fluff of grain, floating like snow
flakes in June. When I look across
the plains to the horizon, it is like we
are in a glass globe someone shook.

The river below meanders without
hurry or rush, secure in the valley floor;
the North Saskatchewan on its way west
or south. This town that flanks the banks
with bright green summer leaves has grown

around two rivers, where the Athabasca
meets the North, accidentally it seems.
But we cannot feel it is a chance meeting.
Something in the landscape, the contours
of geography, made those rivers meet here.

The way the land rises and slants, we think
only God could do this. And right now,
those rivers resemble lives: how the life
of my brother found its way here and now,
the life of my new sister. How they suddenly

run parallel like those two rivers,
and together travel somewhere unknown.
I do not know where those rivers go.
There are treacherous mountains and long
grassland fields and tough ice in winter ahead,

but they seem so strong, so secure like that,
the water so uncompromising and clear.
And now it seems the pollen that floats
in the air all around is like celebration,
like wedding rice some large hand has tossed.

the book of life

as dawn wakes to its slow grey pace again

a small boat crawls across a slate-grey sea
a hummingbird races into the puffy sky

I remember I must choose carefully
if I do not go slowly the green of the leaves will fade

choose the colour of a summer dress
pale blue, pale as mid-morning in May
and the purple of rhododendron blooms

choose the tatters of tarragon for the day
crisp green pepper to awaken the heat
walnut oil and olive oil to dip the bread

walk on the mulch of the rainforest floor
jungle pressing close on all sides
pumas, cougars, bears

choose them carefully or the day will fade

exterminator

after the end of our days
the quiet seems crooked
seems calling out for remorse

I wander about the place unsure
where in the house I hid parts of me
the parts that needed hiding when the earth turned

the garden is abruptly tranquil
I walk it from end to end in surprise

how the hydrangeas have grown giant
the azaleas have spread out after all
the red flowers persist every spring

I guess they were doing that all along
when I was not looking they still bloomed
and grew and rose and opened

as if my questions never mattered
as if the true moments of life remained
locked in the warm brown earth

calling card

the many small ways of being human

removing rust from old windowsills
sandpapering blue paint off the railing
the paint that has peeled off in straggles

once again shining silver goblets never used
once again wiping rain off the veranda tables

moving rose bushes from one spot to another
planting another lilac tree in place of the one lost
yet again watering the everdrooping fuchsias

an endless chore of small services
observations on daily life forever incomplete

the many ways of going on and on

holiday

when the sage met himself in the garden
how did he know who he was?
how do you know such things that cannot be known to you?

the mirrors life puts up for your mind

perhaps it is in the small fetishes
left behind like footsteps in the dirt
how she cannot stop polishing the tarnished silver
how she time and again rearranges the chairs

the dream that wakes him from heavy sleep
the troubled dream of choices not made
how he ends up drinking Scotch in the night

how she falls into tears at the slightest break
how she wrestles the house into the ground

how do you know you are meeting yourself?

how do you know there is another side?

the message

hour falls upon hour
like the heavy footsteps of a mountain troll
lost in its hard thoughts

when I put away the days of obligation
time itself unclasps its hold on the sea
and starts like a beast towards the hills

all the imaginings of the minutes go by
a wild procession of masked and painted birds

everywhere I turn the bright yellow Scotch broom
laughs at my innocence again

yellow flowers, white flowers fly
when the wind picks up and the clouds
fall in with their duvet breath

there is mist, there is fog
there is woodsmoke in the air

Acknowledgements

The following poems from this collection have appeared
in these journals:

"the real postmodern" in *Prairie Fire*

"Sunday afternoon," "Arctic Cathedral," and "street corner"
in *Antigonish Review*

"at the beach" and "quiet of the morning" in *Arc*

"city fog," in *Dandelion Magazine*

"millennium," "the compass," and "La Réunion" in
Contemporary Verse 2

"silence of the country" and "ink stains" in *Poetry Wales*

and "the two rivers" was printed in the church leaflet
containing the wedding ceremony of my brother Örn and
his wife Mary, and the poem was part of the service.

about the author

Kristjana Gunnars is a writer and a professor of writing at the University of Alberta. She has published six books of poetry, including the Coteau Books publication *Exiles Among You*, two short story collections, and five works of prose narrative which merge the genres of fiction and non-fiction, poetry and essay. In this last category is *Zero Hour*, which was a finalist for the Governor General's Award. Her last prose work was *Night Train to Nykøbing*. Her books have also been awarded the Stephan G. Stephansson Award for poetry, the Georges Bugnet Award for fiction, and the McNally-Robinson Award for fiction. In addition to her own writing, Gunnars has edited a collection of short stories by Icelandic Canadians, a collection of scholarly essays on Margaret Laurence, and a book of brief Icelandic folk tales in translation. She has co-edited a publication of modern Icelandic writing.

Born in Iceland, Gunnars moved to Canada in 1969 and has lived in each of the four western Canadian provinces. She currently divides her time between her home on the Sunshine Coast of British Columbia and Edmonton, Alberta.